AUG - - 2011

ERB
8/1'

D1404734

Inside My Body

Why Do My Ears Pop?

Ann Fullick

Raintree

Chicago, Illinois

www.heinemannraintree.com
Visit our website to find out
more information about
Heinemann-Raintree books.

To order:
☎ Phone 888-454-2279
💻 Visit www.heinemannraintree.com
to browse our catalog and order online.

© 2011 Raintree
an imprint of Capstone Global Library, LLC
Chicago, Illinois

All rights reserved. No part of this publication may be
reproduced or transmitted in any form or by any means,
electronic or mechanical, including photocopying,
recording, taping, or any information storage and
retrieval system, without permission in writing from
the publisher.

Edited by Kate de Villiers and Vaarunika Dharmapala
Designed by Steve Mead
Illustrations by KJA-Artists.com
Picture research by Mica Brancic

Originated by Capstone Global Library Ltd
Printed in the United States of America by Worzalla
Publishing

15 14 13 12 11 10
10 9 8 7 6 5 4 3 2 1

Library of Congress Cataloging-in-Publication Data
Fullick, Ann, 1956–
  Why do my ears pop? : hearing / Ann Fullick.
     p. cm. — (Inside my body)
  Includes bibliographical references and index.
  ISBN 978-1-4109-4016-2 (hc) — ISBN 978-1-4109-
4027-8 (pb) 1. Hearing—Juvenile literature. 2. Ear—
Juvenile literature. I. Title. II. Title: Hearing.
  QP462.2.F85 2011
  612.8'5—dc22   2010024682

Acknowledgments
The author and publisher are grateful to the following
for permission to reproduce copyright material: Alamy
pp. **15** (© MedicalRF.com), **19** (© Custom Medical Stock
Photo); Corbis pp. **6** (PhotoAlto/© Laurence Mouton),
22 (© LWA-Sharie Kennedy); Getty Images pp. **7** (AFP/
Berthold Stadler), **17** (Bloomberg), **26** (Taxi/Chris
Clinton); Getty Images news p. **27** (Sandy Huffaker);
iStockphoto.com pp. **4** (© Björn Kindler), **18** (© Roger
Jegg), **20** (© Edward Bock), **24** (© sambrogio); Science
Photo Library pp. **13** (Dr. Richard Kessel & Dr. Gene Shih,
Visuals Unlimited), **16** (CC, ISM), **21** (Medical RF.Com),
25 (CC, ISM); Shutterstock pp. **4 band aid** (© Isaac
Marzioli), **4 gauze** (© Yurok), **8** (Joshua David Treisner), **9**
(© jaana piira), **25 band aid** (© Isaac Marzioli), **25 gauze**
(© Yurok).

Cover photograph of a boy with his fingers in his ears
reproduced with permission of Corbis (© Rob Lewine).

We would like to thank David Wright for his invaluable
help in the preparation of this book.

Every effort has been made to contact copyright holders
of any material reproduced in this book. Any omissions
will be rectified in subsequent printings if notice is given
to the publisher.

Disclaimer
All the Internet addresses (URLs) given in this book were
valid at the time of going to press. However, due to the
dynamic nature of the Internet, some addresses may
have changed, or sites may have changed or ceased to
exist since publication. While the author and publisher
regret any inconvenience this may cause readers, no
responsibility for any such changes can be accepted by
either the author or the publisher.

Contents

Words that appear in the text in bold, **like this**, are explained in the glossary on page 30.

Why Do My Ears Pop?

When you take off in an airplane, walk up a mountain, or dive underwater, your ears can hurt. You cannot hear very well. Then your ears pop, and all is well. Why do your ears pop?

Practical advice

Try some candy!

People often suck on hard candy on a plane as the plane takes off and lands. Sucking and swallowing helps your ears to pop and stops them from hurting. Chewing gum and yawning can help, too.

Air pressure

The **air pressure** inside your ear needs to be the same as the air pressure outside your body. As you land in a plane, the air pressure outside changes, and this can hurt your ear. When you swallow, your **Eustachian tube** opens up and air moves into your ear with a pop. Now you feel better!

You can change the air pressure in your ears. Breath in, hold your nose tightly, close your mouth, and try to push the air gently but firmly down your nose. You should hear your ears go pop!

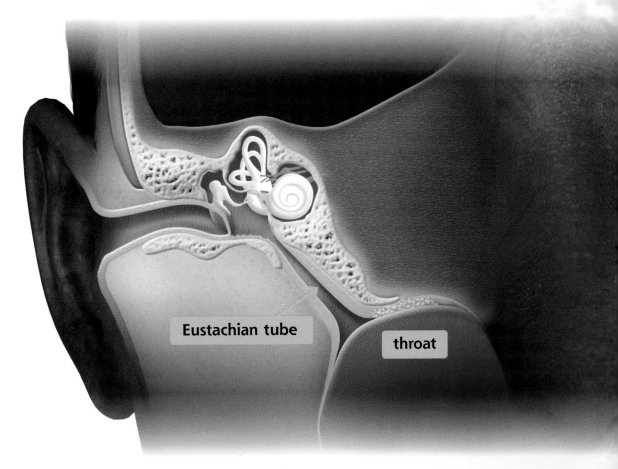

Eustachian tube

throat

🔎 **This is where the Eustachian tube is.**

What Do Ears Do?

Your ears are amazing. You have an outer ear, a middle ear, and an inner ear. In this book you are going to find out what your ears do and how all the different parts work.

🔍 **Your ears help you hear what your friends say.**

Hearing

You hear sound using your ears. Be very quiet and listen. You can hear very quiet sounds, like a cat purring or a clock ticking. You can also hear very loud sounds, such as music or thunder. You talk to your parents, your teachers, and your friends. You can hear signs of danger, such as a car coming down the street. How many times have your ears kept you safe?

Moving

Your ears do more than allow you to hear. Special parts in your inner ear sense when you are moving around. Later, you will find out how this can make you feel dizzy!

Balance

Without your ears you cannot balance well. Your inner ear has senses that tell your brain which way up you are, and whether you are moving your head around. If these do not work properly, you feel very dizzy. You might even fall over or throw up!

Dancers use their ears to hear music, to move, and to balance.

What Is Sound?

If you bang a drum, the skin on the top of the drum **vibrates**. It moves up and down. It pushes the air around it back and forth and makes the air vibrate, too. This is sound. Sound vibrations can travel through air.

🔍 When you pluck a guitar string, you can see the vibrations that make the sound.

Hearing sounds

Sound can also travel through liquids and solids. You can hear sound travel though solids. Put your ear on the table, stretch out your hand, and knock gently on the tabletop.

Your ears can hear sounds in the air best. They do not work so well underwater. Some sounds are so loud that they can hurt your ears—for instance, loud music or a police siren.

Extreme body fact

Loudest animal sounds
Sounds are measured in decibels. One of the loudest animal sounds is made by the blue whale. It is 188 decibels and can travel hundreds of miles underwater. The loudest shout a human can make is about 80 decibels!

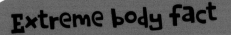 Howler monkeys make loud sounds of about 88 decibels. Their sounds carry through the forest to tell other monkeys where they live.

What Is My Outer Ear?

The outer ear is made up of the **pinna**, the ear canal, and the **eardrum**. The pinnae are the flaps of skin that stick out from either side of your head. Leading from each of these is an ear canal. This is a tube that goes inside your head. At the end of each ear canal is an eardrum, which closes off the outer ear from the middle ear.

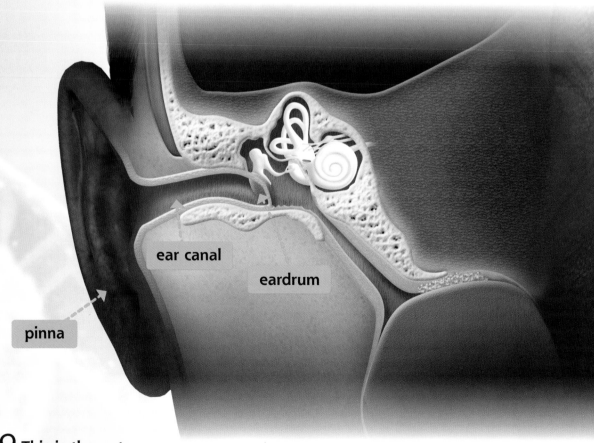

ear canal

eardrum

pinna

🔍 This is the outer ear.

Your eardrum is like a drum skin. When sounds go into your ear, they make your eardrum **vibrate**.

The pinna helps to catch sounds. It also helps you to tell which direction a sound is coming from. Close your eyes and listen. If people talk, you can tell where they are by the sound of their voices!

Ear wax

Your ear makes ear wax to protect the skin inside the ear canal. The wax moves out of your ear, taking any dirt with it. If your ear makes too much wax, it can block your ear and stop you from hearing clearly.

SCIENCE BEHIND THE MYTH

MYTH: Olive oil cures an earache.

SCIENCE: It's true! Doctors have proved that warm oils soften hard earwax so that it comes out—and your ear stops hurting. Your doctor will tell you if this is right for you. It is rather messy, so do not try it at home unless your parents say that you can!

Why Are There Bones in My Ear?

Inside your ear, in your middle ear, you have three small bones known as **ossicles**. They are also called the hammer, the anvil, and the stirrup. When a sound makes your **eardrum vibrate**, this in turn makes the hammer move. The hammer bangs into the anvil, and the anvil moves the stirrup. As the three little bones rock together, they pass the vibration across your middle ear to your inner ear.

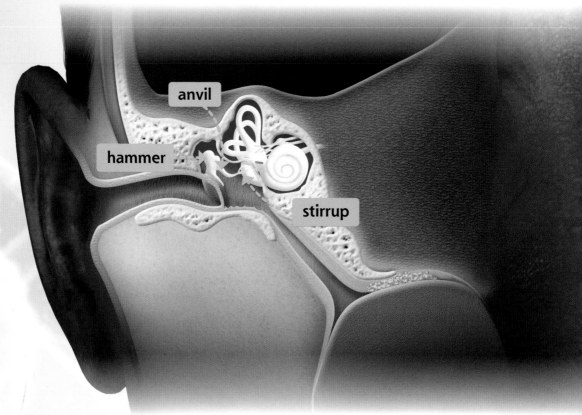

anvil

hammer

stirrup

🔎 **This is the middle ear.**

Your middle ear is usually filled with air. If you get an ear infection, your middle ear may fill up with liquid. When this happens, the little bones cannot rock so well. This means you will not be able to hear as well as usual.

Replacing the bones

Sometimes a person's ear bones can join together or crumble away so that the person cannot hear. Scientists and doctors have made tiny replacement bones from special chemicals. Surgeons operate on the middle ear and put the new "bones" in place. Then the person can hear again!

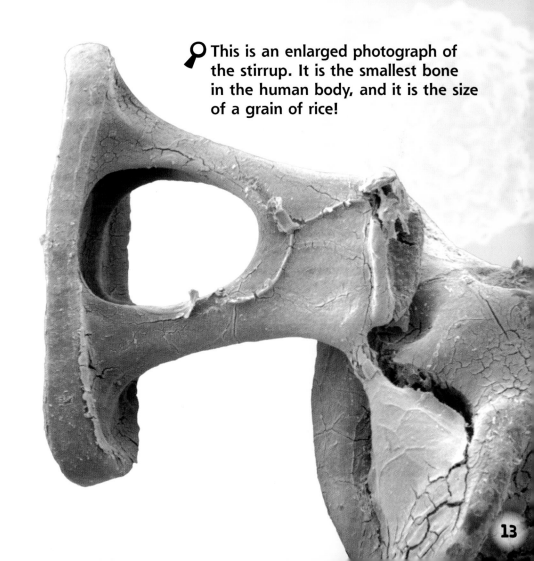

This is an enlarged photograph of the stirrup. It is the smallest bone in the human body, and it is the size of a grain of rice!

How Do I Hear?

Now we are going to look deep inside your ear, right into the inner ear.

You hear because sound vibrations are picked up by **auditory nerves** in your **cochlea**. Vibrations move through the air, from your **eardrum** across the tiny bones of your middle ear to your inner ear. Here they move into the cochlea, which is full of liquid.

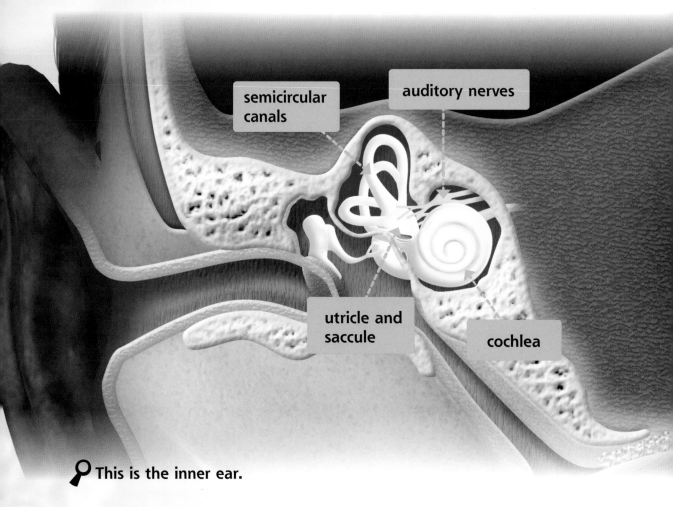

semicircular canals

auditory nerves

utricle and saccule

cochlea

🔍 **This is the inner ear.**

Hairy ears

The sound vibrations move through the liquid like waves. Inside the cochlea there are hairs that join onto nerve endings. As the vibrations move through the liquid, they move the hairs. Nerve messages are sent from the cochlea to the brain. They travel along the auditory nerves.

The messages from the auditory nerves are taken to a special part of your brain. This is how you hear sounds.

Extreme body fact

Hidden length!
Your cochlea is the size of a pea when it is coiled up. If you stretch it out, it is almost 4 centimeters (1.6 inches) long!

The cochlea looks like a snail shell.

What Makes Hearing Difficult?

Hearing is difficult if anything stops sound vibrations from traveling from your outer ear to your inner ear. Wax in your outer ear can do this, as can an ear infection that fills your middle ear with fluid.

Sometimes people get a hole in their **eardrum**. This is called a burst eardrum. It might be because they have hit their head or because they have a middle ear infection. Without an eardrum, a person cannot hear in that ear. All of these problems get better on their own or with treatment from the doctor.

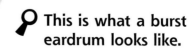

This is what a burst eardrum looks like.

Deafness

If people cannot hear, they are said to be deaf. Some deaf people can hear nothing at all, but others can hear some sounds. Sometimes babies are born deaf. Their **auditory nerves** may not work, or parts of their middle or inner ear may be missing.

Some people can hear when they are born, but lose their hearing later. Bad infections can make people deaf for the rest of their lives. As people get older, their auditory nerves often do not work as well as they used to. This makes hearing difficult.

Hearing aids like this one help people to hear when their own ears do not work very well.

Does Music Hurt My Ears?

Most people enjoy listening to music. But can it hurt your hearing?

At concerts and parties, the sound coming out of the speakers can be so loud that it can damage the little hairs in your **cochlea**. You cannot hear very well for a while afterward. If you are close to the speakers for too long, your ears may not get better.

🔍 **You can enjoy listening to music without damaging your ears. Keep the sound at a safe level.**

MP3 players

MP3 players are great. You can choose your own music and turn it up over the sound of traffic or people talking. But be careful that the music is not so loud that it could damage your ears. Doctors worry that many young people will damage their hearing because they play their MP3 players too loud.

Tinnitus, a constant noise in the ear, is one hearing problem that can be caused by listening to too much loud music.

Extreme body fact

MP3s can hurt!
Sounds of 80 decibels can hurt your ears. Some MP3 players reach 105 decibels, which is as loud as the sound a chainsaw makes!

How Do I Balance?

You can stand on one leg, tilt your head to one side, and look from side to side, all without falling over! How do you keep your balance? Many parts of your body help out, but the **sense organs** in your inner ear are also very important. These organs are the **utricle** and **saccule**, and the **semicircular canals**.

🔍 You can see how well the sense organs work by looking at this gymnast. She is balanced on a beam.

Balancing

The utricle and saccule help you know which way up your head and body are. They also detect when the head is moving forward, backward, or is nodding. The utricle and saccule are filled with fluid and contain jelly-like blobs attached to hairs. When you move around, the fluid and jelly blobs also move and tug on the hairs. This sends a message to your brain, which helps you to keep your balance during movement.

Infection

If you get an infection in the sense organs of your inner ear, you can feel very dizzy, even when you are sitting still. If you stand up, you may feel so dizzy that you fall over! Luckily, this can be easily cured by visiting a doctor.

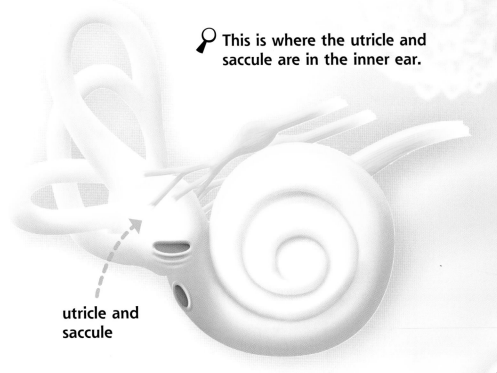

This is where the utricle and saccule are in the inner ear.

utricle and saccule

Why Do I Get Dizzy?

Spin around and around, and then stop. It will feel as if you are still spinning around!

🔍 **Spinning makes you feel dizzy!**

Movement

Your inner ear contains three **semicircular canals**. One goes up, one goes down, and one goes across. As in the **utricle** and **saccule**, each canal is filled with fluid and contains jelly-like blobs attached to hairs. As you move around, the fluid and jelly-like blobs tug on the hairs. This sends a message to your brain. Your brain then knows that you are moving, and the direction that you are moving in.

Dizziness

When you spin around, the fluid in your semicircular canals spins, too. When you stop spinning, the liquid keeps going. Your eyes tell your brain you are not moving, but your semicircular canals tell your brain you are spinning around. This is why you feel dizzy! As soon as the liquid in your semicircular canals stops moving, you stop feeling dizzy.

Extreme body fact

Dizzy dancers
Dancers spin around a lot, but they do not get dizzy. How? Dancers stare at one spot and then spin their head in a quick move. Their head stays in one place most of the time. This stops dancers from getting dizzy.

🔍 **This is where the semicircular canals are in the inner ear.**

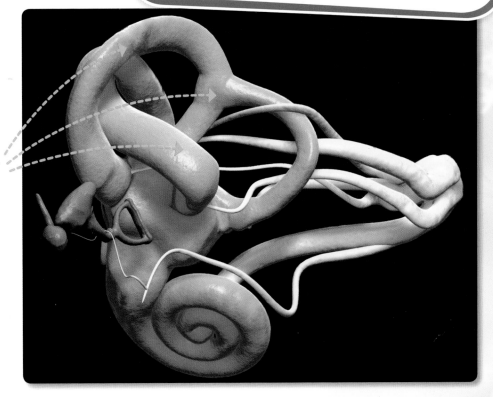

semicircular canals

How Can I Take Care of My Ears?

If you take care of your ears, you can help to protect your hearing. Here are some useful tips:

- Keep your ears clean and dry.
- Never poke things into your ears. You might hurt your **eardrum**.
- Listen to music sensibly. Remember that very loud music can make it harder for you to hear well.
- Water in dirty swimming pools can carry germs and cause infection. When you go swimming, protect your ears with earplugs.

🔍 This boy is making sure his earplugs are in place while he plays in a swimming pool.

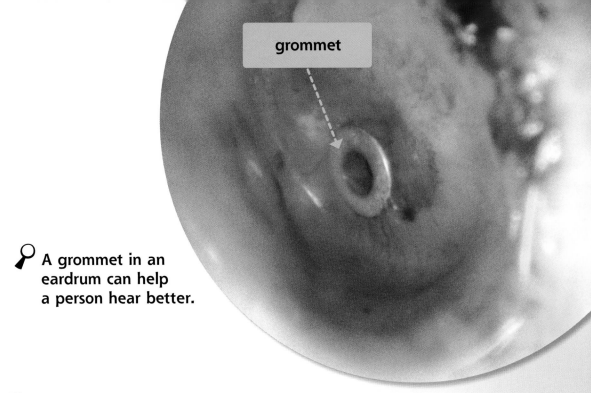

grommet

 A grommet in an eardrum can help a person hear better.

Glue ear

Some children have a problem called glue ear. This is when too much fluid gets into the middle ear and cannot flow down the **Eustachian tube**. The problem is fixed using grommets. These are small, plastic valves that allow the fluid to drain out through the eardrum until the Eustachian tube grows big enough to work on its own.

SCIENCE BEHIND THE MYTH

MYTH: Earwigs can climb into your ears and eat your brain.

SCIENCE: No, they can't! Earwigs do not climb into human ears. However, doctors do find many strange things in children's ears, such as food, beads, small toys, and insects. The child has usually put the object in his or her own ear!

Ears Are Amazing!

On each side of your head you have an ear. They are full of surprises! You have an outer ear, a middle ear, and an inner ear.

Sound, balance, and movement

Your outer ear catches sound and takes it into the rest of your ear. Your middle ear contains small bones that carry the sound waves into your inner ear.

Your ears let you hear everything from a whisper to a warning shout. Hearing is a very precious sense.

Your inner ear holds the **cochlea**, the part that is sensitive to sounds. It also contains the **utricle**, **saccule**, and the **semicircular canals**. These help you to balance, and to know where your body is and when you are moving!

Every time you talk to your friends, or stand on your head, or enjoy the dizzy feeling after a ride at an amusement park, remember to thank your ears. They are truly amazing!

Your ears tell you which way up you are, even on a roller coaster!

All About Ears

A dog's squeaky toy can make a sound of 135 decibels. That is loud enough to damage your hearing if the squeaking goes on too long.

Your ears continue to grow throughout your life. They grow almost 2 millimeters (0.08 inch) every nine years!

Modern hearing aids are very small and can be hidden inside or behind your ear (see page 17). In the 1800s and early 1900s, people used ear trumpets to help them hear. These were big— often 30 centimeters (1 foot) long!

Some people have hissing, roaring, clicking, or ringing noises in their ears all the time. They are not imagining things. They have a condition called tinnitus (see page 19).

An Indian man named Anthony Victor has the longest recorded hair growing out of his ears. It is 18.1 centimeters (7.12 inches) long!